The
WAY OF THE SERVANT

*This Book
is lovingly dedicated
to you, the reader,
for your willingness
to become the light
that lights the world.*

*Jeshua is the original Aramaic name for Jesus. It is the name
that he uses with Jayem the beginning of their communion.*

The
WAY OF THE SERVANT

Living the Light of Christ

Enlightenment: The Final Stage

Jeshua

Copyright © 2019 by Audio Enlightenment Press All rights reserved. No part of this publication may be reproduced, distributed, or transmitted in any form or by any means, including photocopying, recording, or other electronic or mechanical methods, without the prior written permission of the publisher, except in the case of brief quotations embodied in critical reviews and certain other non-commercial uses permitted by copyright law. Printed in the United States of America

0 1 2 3 4 5 6 7 8 9

First Printing, December 2019
ISBN 978-1-941489-44-4

WayofMastery.com

WayofMasteryBooks.com

Kindle/ePub / Audiobooks
Available on WayofMasteryBooks.com

First "AudioEnlightenmentPress.Com" Printing
December 2019

CONTENTS

Foreword .... *i*
Preface .... *vii*
Book One *13*
Book Two *39*
Book Three *63*
Book Four *83*
After Wards *95*
Epilogue *105*

Foreword

By Jayem

You have in your hands The Way of the Servant, the second of the five core texts of The Way of Mastery Pathway, created in a cohesive series of books for the first time. All five are given in the order the teachings were revealed, and each of these is equally important, for they are exactly how Jeshua meticulously set about to restore His teachings and build His Pathway.

Here, He is describing, in the most succinct, direct, and even poetic language, not the beginning of our journey, nor processes that serve us on it, but, rather, the last and final stage. He is revealing the end of our transformation, as though lifting us from a forest path up an unknown mountain to glimpse the summit, before gently placing us back down and taking the necessary steps, with us!

And so, only as we truly surrender to the deep and transfiguring ways of enlightenment, only as we become lived into all He conveys about serving Love, through the larger body of teachings of The Way of Mastery Pathway, can we become capable of recognizing the depth and wisdom He conveys here.

Every word in *The Way of the Servant* is saturated in, and conveys a profound 'encoding', or spiritual transmission. They quite literally 'plants seeds' deep in our unconscious, igniting a Light so deep that it pulls us, like a magnet, through all the stages of healing and growth that yet lay before us, always according to our readiness and willingness. And this comes, in ripe time, from our desire to 'return Home in God', to truly know fully the answer to the one question we all share:

'Who am I, truly?'

He began this, in many ways with A Course In Miracles, and The Way of Mastery continues what He began there. The Way of the Servant launches the next significant phases of His Atonement and enlightenment process.

For, as He shares, "There is a journey to the Kingdom, and a journey within it." And while forgiveness fulfills the corrective phase of a return to The Kingdom, the alchemy that will truly and fully flower the soul's journey *within* it is revealed in *The Way of the Servant*.

It is from this foundation that He would then come to launch the formal three year curriculum of *The Christ Mind Trilogy* comprised of

~*The Way of the Heart*
~*The Way of Transformation* and
~*The Way of Knowing*.

Therefore, keep in mind, as you read The Way of the Servant, that because He is describing and transmitting these seeds with the end in mind, and because its purpose is not quite the same as providing, as He does later, teachings to gently guide and deepen our studentship, what you find in these pages may jostle you, or even feel a bit uncomfortable. It may seem too cryptic, or even blunt.

Foreword

So, I would advise to just bring your attention to your breath first, finding stillness within, and simply notice as you relax and immerse in these teachings, what does arise as feeling states for you? What thoughts seem to erupt in the mind? For the light of the seeds being planted will already be working within the depths of your being.

I know it was this way with me, as I first encountered these teachings, just after they were transcribed by Him, in a little red notebook I carried with me everywhere at that time. I confess that I hated the drudgery of carrying that damn red notebook!

And I hated how what He was saying was fomenting within me, churning up things I was not comfortable with, well before I was capable of understanding that this was just my experience of my own ego being confronted, and feeling like a cornered cat. There is a Wisdom within its teachings of such infinite depth, which so brilliantly reveals, in good time, what we ourselves will grow to see, to know, and *to be* in all aspects of living. For *The Way of the Servant* brings us to the realized experience in space-time, and via the body-mind, of all He would lead us to.

I call this the *Seamless Life*. When realized, it is for you, the student, an uncompromised life of power and astonishing flow, where your devotion is your practice, your service, your career, your reason for rising in the morning, and is as well, the fulfillment of your deepest longing, the lived answer to that question: 'Who am I, truly?'

And it will feel that life is living you, not you living it!

All things will feel long ago forgiven. The deepest fears embraced and suffused in Love. There will be a mystery

The Way of the Servant

moving you, invisibly like the wind, in ways often impossible to be understood, and not simply by others around you, but even by yourself! And yet, and yet…there is perfect trust, perfect surrender, and the constancy of eternal gratitude for the grace that answered your deepest prayer, and brought you *Home*.

And this will occur right here, right now, in the very conditions and world you once struggled with. And all things reveal Holy Perfection, Holy Love, Holy Vision, and an exquisite harmony and orchestration, revealing all of a Whole and Holy that Life shares but one purpose: to see that God IS, God is only Love, and only Love is real; not 'there then', but 'here, always and eternally'May all beings be freed of their illusion and truly know Who is the breath of their breath, the reason of their existence, and the Love that moves through them to heal, comfort, nurture, and bless His creation. And in this does Heaven come to Earth. As He put it in *A Course in Miracles*:

'Heaven and Earth will pass away means only that they will cease to exist as separate states.' Here, then, is the culmination of the Vision of the Christ Path, and the book you now hold reveals for you this culmination both in your own unfolding, and in that of humanity.

Lastly, I want to point out that, like *The Jeshua Letters*, what He teaches here was scribed. The channeling phase was in the future, neatly hidden from me, for He knew that fear would have totally overwhelmed me, and fear defeats the goal of the student's true healing and waking into Christ Mind.

The loving teacher, which Jeshua clearly is, knows this, and learns to speak the language of the student, so that love may transform, and fear be defeated.

Foreword

Love seems to already know the map each soul will need to travel, with twists and turns designed specifically and uniquely for each of us. And Love unravels and awakens us, from the cobwebs of our own chosen 'dream of the dreamer, itself.'

Blessings to you!

Jayem
December, 2019

Preface

It is August 8, 1990. Not far beyond a tiny town on the southwestern coast of the island of Hawaii, a narrow road winds down from the highway to a lovely little spot named Keokea. The coastline here is rugged. Battered cliffs of reds and browns plunge from treeline to sea. There is a jetty of sorts that runs from the end of the northernmost cliffs. A crude pile of boulders, it creates a shallow lagoon just right for small children to swim in. There is no white sand beach and, thank God, no throng of tourists baking in the delicious Hawaiian sun.

Near the center of the park a stream meanders through the dense foliage. Here I bathed yesterday, making my way far enough upstream to be out of sight. I dipped my body into the cool waters, then sat on a rock, allowing the warm caress of a gentle breeze to dry me, breathing deeply the sweet fragrance of plumeria.

Here, in this magical spot that evokes memories of Eden from some forgotten place of the soul, meditation comes easily. In no time at all, I feel that familiar place, as though I have come to the eye of the hurricane, "the stillpoint of the turning world."

A familiar vibration; He is here. As though waiting for me to return Home from a journey, He knocks gently, assuredly, on the door of my heart. I answer, turning my attention to Him, and Him alone. *It is time for us to begin our second work together. For this did I suggest the notebook.* (He refers to a small red binder that I impulsively threw into my shopping cart a few days ago.) *Use this solely for our communications. The publication of 'The Jeshua Letters' is now imminent.* (A series of events, none of which I could have imagined, would begin within a month that did, indeed, lead to the book's publication.)

The Way of the Servant

Again, I suggest that you continue in your learning of trust. It is not important that you see how all things will be accomplished. Remember, to the world the awakened mind seems naive, but the opinions of those who believe what is Real, is not, and what is not Real, is, surely should not be heeded.

I am distracted. The mosquitoes have won. Sighing, I rise from the rock, dress, and return to camp...

One of the reasons I love Hawaii so much is this moment. The sun has long since set, replaced by a bright, full moon. It illuminates trees and rocks and ocean waves, while painting cloud edges in silver- white, and still it is warm! Warm enough to lay here undressed, drinking the energies of this place deep into every cell.

As, again, I feel His presence within me, a thought of amazement arises in my mind. He is continuing our conversation now as if there was no break in our communication. This simple fact is a gentle reminder that time is somehow not quite what I have learned it is. As He speaks, I *see* it, the title:

The Way of the Servant

Living the Light of Christ

"For the first shall be last, and the last, first."

This teaching was not intended for the use it has been given by those who would find in me justification for the judgment of their brothers and sisters. That which is called the sacred book of your Bible does,

Preface

in fact, contain many seeds of wisdom. However, these have often been separated from their original contexts and woven into stories designed to serve not the Holy Father, but the **conception** of God the mind in separation would long for.

I gave this teaching to those known as my disciples. Its meaning serves as the theme of this present work, for when the mind is truly awakened from the dream of separation and the soul is returned to its only Reality as the Son of God, there comes then a new beginning. No longer is there futile searching for what the world cannot offer or hope to contain.

Abiding in that peace which forever passes understanding, the soul is at rest. It neither desires the things of the world nor judges them. It learns the sublime art of what has been called "waiting on the Lord." This merely means that the soul moves in accordance with the Father's will, and can no longer consider doing otherwise. The soul dons the cloak of the servant.

The Way emerges for us: When the acknowledgment of your Reality as the only begotten Son of God is accomplished and the Armageddon between this Reality and the habit of useless dreams is ended, the journey to the Kingdom is completed and the journey **within** it begins. The whole of Creation is reclaimed as **one's own**, and the soul's only desire is that Creation be restored as a reflection of the holy thought of God, who is but Love.

Love is a radiant splendor forever shining beyond all appearance, a splendor held as a distant memory in the heart of all forms of Life, and it is this that Life strains to rediscover. When this is accomplished, the very purpose of Creation will be completed, and the things of Heaven and Earth shall pass away, as mist before the rising sun.

In this work, I shall address the meaning of servantship, for here is found the highest calling of the soul, as well as the final enactment possible in the field of manifestation.

The Way of the Servant

True servantship is not in any way possible while yet there lingers hope for salvation in the things of the world, including those ideas of salvation which cleverly conceal the fear that is ego; the dream of the separate self that can gain, or lose.

I will clarify the true nature of the servant, as well as the qualities of genuine service. We will journey through the field of obstacles which peep the highest joy just beyond the grasp of the one who would join in union with God.

Know this: Nothing ever imagined by the mind of man can bring the soul such depth of peace, such breadth of fulfillment, such heights of unspeakable joy as can servantship. Enlightenment, when fully realized, gives birth to the servant as surely as does the flower burst forth from the seed well planted and nurtured.

Contemplate deeply what is here being spoken, again and yet again, in the quiet of solitude, for these words I have chosen deliberately. Taking them deep into your heart will hasten your consummate awakening.

This work is given to assist those who will soon touch the heart of a perfect Remembrance. It is a great truth that greater works than mine shall you who serve Love bring forth into the world in these Last Days.

Herein is the introduction completed...

After giving the introduction, He suggested I be patient because this work would come into form at the appropriate time. He also asked that I keep the little red notebook close at hand, and I agreed. I had no way of knowing then that three years would pass before He would finish it!

Preface

The process of writing was actually quite simple. I dragged the notebook with me wherever I went, lived my life, and waited. Sometimes, several months would go by without so much as a mention of this work from Him. At times He literally stopped in mid-sentence, only to pick it up later as if there had been no interruption.

Waking me at two or three in the morning with that familiar little vibration in my heart continued to be one of his apparently favorite times. Finally, I grew accustomed to the fact that He might never finish it at all! I confess that my wife occasionally enjoys telling friends how I threw the notebook across the room when the words I was scribing pushed my buttons, or conveniently left it on a friend's table, "forgetting" what I had done with it.

In fact, when He dictated the final few pages and said "Amen," it failed to sink in that it was done. I got out of my chair to head to the kitchen, suddenly stopped in my tracks, and muttered, "It's done. No more little red notebook!"

Alan Cohen, in his foreword to *The Jeshua Letters*, called Jeshua "a masterful teacher." Looking back, this one simple fact becomes abundantly clear. *The Way of the Servant* is a link in an exquisite tapestry being woven by this loving master, always dedicated to awakening us all to the presence and reality of Love, beyond our fears and hurts and angers and doubts.

The Way of the Servant, like a good painting, reveals its treasures to you the longer you linger with it. It has pushed my deepest buttons, showing me where my own ego games continue, requiring my attention. It has become an ever-present reminder that He is with all of us always, overflowing with the Love we are choosing to remember on this planet.

The Way of the Servant

We offer it to you as it was offered to us. If you choose, it will become a blessing on your journey, a constant companion righting your course whenever, for a fleeting moment, you are tempted to be distracted by the voice of the world that seems to have made a home in your mind. As this gift from Jeshua has done for so many, may it also serve to turn your ear to the gentle Voice that yet lives within us all, the Voice which speaks only of Love, of what we are together, forever. Streams of joy!

Jayem
Ubud, Bali
April 2006

Book One

The Way of the Servant

Book One

Servantship.
It appears an odd word,
yet within it lies the meaning of sacrifice,
of Love,
of true Being.

Servantship is a *vocation*
to which one is called,
not by a God who exists apart from you,
but by that one true God
who abides eternally
in the Heart of one's heart,
and is forever the Soul of one's soul.

For the one true God
is your only Reality,
and in this does the recognition dawn
that *you* —
who would insist
on the smallness of yourself
as you have dreamt it to be —
contain, in truth, all wisdom;
that *you*
contain all perfections
holy men would so diligently seek
and ignorant men would mistakenly seek
in the destitution
of their worldly dreams.

That one true God
to whom you are eternally united,
so that no boundary between you

The Way of the Servant

can be distinguished,
is that which has sustained
the infinite forms
of your dreams,
their incessant creation fueled
by the one thought of separation.

And now,
in the time of Recognition,
after the allure of the dream has paled
and finally lost all trace of significance,
and in that perfect silence
where the sleeping Son no longer rebels
against the simple
and loving
embrace of the Holy Father,
the light of the living Christ is rekindled.

As a flame in a windless place,
its light grows ever brighter,
dissolving all traces of the shadows
which have kept it hidden,
lighting up the dark places
where the dust which is the world
has settled,
until even the dust is dissolved
and becomes as Light itself.

The doer is undone.
The maker of the world is unmade,
and Christ again,
lives.

Here,
the end of all fruitless journeying.

Book One

Here,
the ceasing of all strife.

Here,
the realization of the only Truth,
beyond all utterance,
beyond the understanding of the world,
beyond even the dream
of the one who would seek God.

For the seeker is no more,
as if he had never been,
save as a fading memory of a dream
dreamt long ago.

Returned to the embrace
of our Holy Father,
the one who has returned acknowledges:
"I AM that One."

Christ lives, and Christ alone.

As it is,
has been,
and forever shall be.

The awakened Heart
is likened unto one,
who has journeyed,
to the summit
of the highest mountain.

The Way of the Servant

Here,
she looks out upon
the distances traveled,
the many landscapes
stretching out below her,
the seemingly infinite shapes and hues.

She beholds all the worlds of mankind,
and sees them as empty,
as a moment's diversion,
fragments of but one dream.
She beholds herself as the one dreamer,
and she would that
every vestige of herself
be nudged from sleep to waking.

And now,
the transformation is completed.

Resting in the Light of Remembrance,
embraced eternally
in the arms of his Father,
the only begotten Son abides
in the Kingdom
prepared for him
in that most ancient
beginning before time is.

Her will has become
as her Father's.
United again as one,
the first movement of that Divine Will
stirs in the vision before her.
Compassion arises
for the whole of Creation

and she sees without effort
the task set before her:
the awakening of the whole of herself,
now recognized as every soul,
every blade of grass,
every wisp of breeze.

Awakened
as the source of all things,
existing in all things,
the one Son,
united with the Holy Father —
the brief dream of the Prodigal Son
vanquished —
looks out upon himself
with but one desire: Awaken!

Restored to her rightful place
at the right hand of the Holy Father,
purified of all distortions
born of a moment's dream,
a movement begins.
Felt in the heart,
it expands first upward,
upward beyond the crown of the head,
then outward,
filling every cell
of a body transfigured,
brought evermore
to the form of a vehicle
that will serve only the fulfillment
of her task.

And then,
when the Father and the Son together

have prepared
the body and mind of Christ,
the movement of Divine Will
becomes *downward*,
compelling the arisen Christ to step
deliberately and without haste
in the direction of all that now lies
before Him,
far below Him,
spread as far as the eye can see,
slumbering at the base
of this great Mount Zion.

Now,
her steps
become more certain.

Now,
his steps
become ever lighter,
unburdened from the weight
of a self that never was,
yet clamored for a food
which never satisfied.

Now,
her steps
become ever more directed
from a source perfectly trusted,
and with each step,
dissolving
is any need to know
where she goes,
what she shall eat,
or what she shall wear,

Book One

for her Father knows
she has need of these things.

He knows but one thing only:
he goes as the wind,
caring not the direction of his travels,
remembering not
the direction of his coming,
abiding always
in the Light of the Holy Father.

Behold!
The servant is born.

*For the first shall be last,
and the last, first.*

The only begotten Son dreams.
And in his dream is forgotten
that which eternally
he *is*.

And the first has become last,
even as the creation
of innumerable worlds arises,
replacing the splendor
of Remembrance
with the lifeless,
enchanting,
ever-changing forms of mere illusions.
And the last has become as the first.

The Way of the Servant

Yet,
within the worlds
of her dream
lies the crystal clear gem
of Reality,
for the unspeakable Love
which the Father is
illuminates the dream of the Son,
granting her perception
of all that she would *choose* to perceive.

And the Father merely waits,
abiding wholly in the purity of his Light,
seeing naught but the splendor
of his Son,
waiting for the one who lays dreaming
to awaken.

The first is, indeed,
now last,
and what must always be last —
mere illusions cast by,
and within,
the mind of the Son —
has become first:
the Kingdom is forgotten.

Habituated
to the play of shadows,
no more than projections
of his momentary thought,
the Son suffers the worlds
of his own making,
reveling in transitory pleasures,
enduring the pain of countless wounds;

yet he continues on,
proliferating the worlds of experience,
seeking ever more desperately
for what he has long forgotten,
knowing not what it is he seeks,
calling it by various names,
striving endlessly
to discover his salvation
in the worlds he has made,
insisting it be found there.

And the Father waits,
abiding in the purity of his Light,
seeing naught but the radiant splendor
of his Son.

The maker of the world,
but not of Reality,
unknowingly remains impelled
to experience again and yet again
the fruit of pride:
vanity of vanities.

Insisting on her chosen thought,
enmeshed
in a deepening web of shadow,
yet she cries out desperately
in the aloneness of her soul:
"*I am,*
I create,
My will be done!"

And still,
the Father waits,
abiding in the purity of his Light,

seeing naught but the radiant splendor
of his beloved Son.

As the offspring of Light Divine
wanders from world to world,
ceaselessly moved to act,
seeking
without knowing he seeks,
searching for the Kingdom
without knowing he searches,
creating and devouring the forms
of his apparently endless dream,
an impulse begins to grow.

At first unnoticed,
soft,
and seemingly far away,
overwhelmed by the noise and conflicts
of his making,
it grows.

Through endless circles
and a myriad of landscapes,
ceaselessly
through agonies and ecstasies
disguised in infinite masks,
it grows,
becoming as a Voice
whispering beyond the threshold
of his hearing,
whispering a song
forever eternal,
forever untouched by a single jot or tittle
of all that the Son experiences.

It is a song
of Truth beyond all doubt,
a song
of Reality uncompromised,
a song
which sings of the imperishable essence,
the very essence of his being,
a song which is
the Love of the Holy Father.

Though the Voice sings the song
without ceasing,
the Son hears not,
her ears turned not
to the Voice whose song
is like one crying in the wilderness,
but to the din
of ephemeral shadows
cast upon the walls of her prison,
recognizing not the Light
which lights all darkness,
believing still that darkness to be
the Light she would seek,
the Light that will illuminate her way,
and reveal the treasure
she believes resides there.

And still,
the Father waits,
abiding in the purity of his Light,
seeing naught but the radiant splendor
of his only begotten,
his beloved,
his Son,
eternal.

The Way of the Servant

Still,
the Son travels.
Through valleys
of the shadow of death,
climbing mountains
made of the stones of uncertainties,
fording rivers whose far shores
often cannot be seen,
rivers wild with the tumult of emotions
arising like angry waves
from depths already seething
in memories
clutched tightly in the grasp
of the one who believes in shadow
and worships it,
knowing not that he does so.

And still, the Father waits,
abiding always in the purity of his Light,
rejoicing in the perfection of his Son,
waiting for the child
to make but one simple,
quiet choice:
to awaken!

As she travels on,
there comes now a moment here,
and again there,
moments sadly fleeting,
yet filled with the clarity
of the song that calls unto her.
Were she to turn but for an instant
and embrace what the moment would offer,
the journey would be no more,
the simple choice recognized,

and made.

It is but his weariness
that forces him to pause,
to rest in that silence
which is the doorway to his Heart,
where alone fulfillment resides.

The treasure rests
in the palm of her hand,
yet she comprehends it not.

Habituated only
to the grasping of illusion,
she has not the capacity
to recognize what has touched her:
the Light of the Father
that would loosen the knot
binding her to enchantment
with unceasing emptiness.
Believing himself restored,
and himself the restorer,
he plunges headlong once again,
going on,
going — where?

He mistakes his endless circling
for clear direction to the finality
he would make,
failing to see he travels
but the same valleys,
the same mountains,
the same rivers.

Cleverly cloaking these

with her own shifting perceptions,
she beguiles herself into believing
not that she sees differently,
but that what she sees
is different and new.

And yet the Father waits,
ever so patient
with his beloved Son,
abiding eternally in the knowledge
beyond comprehension,
that the dream his Son would dream
in truth, exists not;
rejoicing without ceasing
in the radiance of his holy child,
untouched eternally
by the illusion of sin.

A deepening weariness grows
in the heart of the dreamer,
a weariness
neither understood
nor recognized
by the mind accustomed to shadows,
nor a body blind
to the seed of Light within it.

The dreamer moves on,
yet the weariness remains within him,
unvanquished by his fruitless pause,
restored not by his habitual escape
from shadows.

Disconcerted,
she moves along familiar byways,

increasingly unable to blot out
this persistent
though subtle
weariness,
an ache that remains with her,
no matter the form
or intensity
of her efforts to be free of it.

And now,
fear arises.
It is a fear unlike
any he has experienced
within his countless journeys
in the fields of illusions.
Not a fear
from which he can hide,
nor a fear
he can successfully suppress
by heaping upon it
the weight of evermore enchantments.

It is a fear
to which she is unaccustomed,
for it stems not
from her experience of the world,
but grows quietly from
and remains present within
the core of her being.

Intensifying his efforts
to find solace in the changing landscapes
of his dreams
serves only to confirm
the reality of his fear.

The Way of the Servant

Unlike anything
she has yet encountered,
this fear becomes a constant
though unwelcome
companion.
It becomes as a child
who increasingly refuses to be ignored,
and the dreamer of a thousand worlds,
proud author
of a multitude of illusions,
survivor of numerous heavens and hells,
trembles.

In his trembling,
he does not pause in his vain pursuits
as much as he is *made* to stop,
and looking at
what he would resist seeing,
he beholds:
The salt of the world
has begun to lose its savor.

Weariness
perceived as fear
appears to her as an unknown force
from which she cannot hide,
yet cannot embrace.
It seems to run before her
as she scampers first up one hill,
greeting her face-to-face at the summit,
and fording rivers
swum countless times before,
she emerges only to find it
waiting on the far shore.

Book One

Beginning to sense
that this unknown force
is not to be cast aside,
the dreamer laments within himself,
and in the midst of all his doing,
the faint echo of a sound
he has forever dreaded
is heard.

The doer of all deeds is shaken,
the foundation of his creations
wobbles and weakens;
he beholds the force within himself
and,
for the first time,
acknowledges his impending death.
Though she acts within her worlds,
striving to continue
in the only way she knows,
seeking fervently
to return and remain
in familiar terrain,
the forms of her dream
hold not their enticing allure,
and her efforts to remain
in all that she knows
provide no satisfaction.
Her thirst is not fulfilled,
and even her sleep is troubled.

The dreamer,
saddened by the growing loss of luster
beheld in his dreams,
becomes as one who grasps at mirages,
finding naught but emptiness

in his hands,
yet continues to grasp
because it is all he knows to do.

She waits for a death
she is sure will come,
both loathing it
and secretly longing for it.
She is defeated
but knows not how,
nor by what.
The dreams,
that throughout countless lifetimes
had fed him with the promise
of fulfillment,
wither,
like parched leaves clinging to branches
whose source of water
is mysteriously severed from unseen roots,
while the power of his life
drains from his limbs.

The proud dreamer
has not the energy to dream,
and believes beyond question
that where there are not dreams,
there is not Life,
and the growing emptiness
is as a torment to him.

She raises her head only occasionally,
and feebly,
hoping to the end to see in her dreams
the Life she had always sought there.

Book One

Finally,
wearied to the bone
of fighting what he senses
but cannot see,
of what he feels
but cannot grasp,
the dreamer releases not only
the last vestige of his will to dream,
but lays down
even the dream of the dreamer,
and dissolves into what he knows
must certainly be
his final, and consummate,
death.

*And the first shall be last,
and the last, first.*

And now,
the dreamer is laid to rest.
It is a rest
from which there can be
no hope of arising.

Unlike the many pauses
in which the maker of all worlds
merely retreated to gain strength
for his journeys,
this rest
transcends the world.
It transcends the body,
the mind,
and all the dreamer

had thought himself to be.

It is a rest
in which even the soul reclines,
turned away
from all enchantments,
dissolved in the Mystery of all mysteries,
beyond the pale of words,
beyond all imagined things.

Verily,
the dreamer
is no more to be found.
Vanished without a trace,
not only of her ending,
but of her beginning;
the journey which *seemed* to be,
is *not*.

And the last,
made to be first,
is again become last.
Not by a force which comes
from outside the dreamer,
but a force which already abides
in the very seed
of the dreamer's beginning;
the certainty of his death
is present in his birth
and must inevitably flower,
its petals blotting out
the very dream of the dreamer itself.

Yet what is perceived
by the dreamer

as the darkness of certain death,
the giving up of all hope for salvation
in the things of the worlds
she has conjured into being,
is not darkness,
but Light.

It is that Light which lights all things,
the echo of an endless song
coming as a thief in the night,
the eternal voice of our Holy Father.

And the Voice
has overcome
the shouting of the world,
restoring the Son
to a rest true and deep,
a rest which alone can heal and transform
the heart of his holy Son.

The one who would be
the dreamer of all worlds rests,
unseen by a world
unaware of what occurs in its midst,
all boundaries
that have defined her form
dissolved in incomprehensible Light.

The Son abides
in the rest of perfect Grace.

What was last
and made first
is again made last.
And all the heavens rejoice

beyond the capacity of the world
to hear.

And now is the world,
entranced by the power of its dreams,
lifted gently toward
the open arms of God.

At the end of a holy instant,
incapable of measurement
by a world imprisoned in time,
the rest of the only begotten
Son of God
gives rise to a movement
not born of a mind
bound to the illusion of separation,
but of the eternal Heart
of the arisen Christ,
a movement that would take him
not back into the dream of the world,
but ever deeper
into the Reality of his being:
a journey within the Kingdom of Heaven.

Awakened,
the mind free
from the shackles of want,
the body free
from useless demands
made by a self that never was,
a heart beating only
by the breath of the Most High,
the arisen Christ moves
where once the world arose,
seeing naught but the glory

of his Father's Kingdom:
radiance beyond description,
joy without boundary,
purpose in which
fulfillment is certain.

Here,
no trace of effort
is to be found.

Here,
no taint of striving
clouds his perception.

Here,
no constriction of the heart
by the grand illusion of fear
is felt.

Reduced to simplicity,
exalted above all things,
the one transformed
by the miracle of Grace
lives and walks.
Behold!
The dreamer,
now transformed,
is reborn as the one
through whom the Father alone
works to transfigure the world.
For darkness shall become as Light,
extended without end
until Creation itself is no more.
Indeed,
the first is again, first.

As it was in the beginning,
is now,
and forever shall be.

The Prodigal Son
is returned,
and all of Heaven is shaken
by the praise of the Heavenly Host;
the Father and the Son
rest together as one
in that peace which forever passes
all understanding.

To any among you
who has ears to hear,
let her hear.

And all things *are* made new.

Book Two

The Way of the Servant

Servantship.
It appears an odd word,
yet within it lies the meaning of sacrifice,
of Love,
of true Being.

What, then,
can we say of sacrifice?
The cloak of ignorance
has been cast off,
the darkness of a solitary thought
dissolved in the simple brilliance
of a Light far brighter
than ten thousand suns,
and the soul of one
who has seen through the vanity
of useless wandering
is again restored
to the place from which
it has not ever ventured forth.

The holy one
is again become first,
and sees that nowhere
is there to be found a second.

I AM the first-born of my Father,
standing before all things.
Moving not,
I travel far.
Embracing all things, I touch myself.

*Creation arises within me.
I AM the first and the last,
the alpha and omega.*

*Fulfilled beyond all measure,
I need nothing.
Possessing the whole of Creation,
I desire nothing.*

*That which has been,
I AM.
That which is,
I AM.
That which shall be,
I AM.*

*Looking far,
I behold not my ancient beginning.
Gazing near,
I see not my end.*

*I AM a circle of heavenly Light
embracing all things,
knowing all things,
allowing all things.*

*My splendor
fills the vastness of space
and is contained
between two thoughts.*

*The wind is birthed
from my holy breath,
and carries my glory
to all far places.*

*I AM the power
by which all dreams are dreamt.*

*I AM the purpose
of all actions performed.*

*I AM the Way,
the Truth, and the Life,
and the whole of Creation
returns to the Father through me.*

*I AM the praying,
the prayer,
and the answer.*

*I AM the dream,
the dreamer,
and her awakening.*

*I AM the sin,
the sinner,
and the salvation.*

*I AM the vast ocean
from which
the dew drop arises.*

*I AM the tear
on the cheek of a newborn
who brings me into form and time.*

*I AM the words
before your eyes,
the writer,
and the one who even now reads.*

The Way of the Servant

*I AM the one dreamer
bold enough to imagine
the illusion of separation,
and the one worthy
of releasing the allure of sleep.*

*I AM,
simply, that,
I AM.*

It is this
that the awakened Son proclaims,
without a trace of thought
to obscure the brilliance and purity
of his being.

She looks for herself,
and sees only
the Father.

He reaches to himself,
and embraces only
the whole of Creation.

The glass,
once filled with a momentary thought
of imaginary sustenance,
is again
become the emptiness
overflowing with living waters.

The holy chalice
is raised to her lips.
She drinks eternally,
and is satisfied.

Herein
is the meaning of sacrifice:
Never has there existed
what must be eternally unreal,
and what is not
can be neither lost
nor sacrificed.

What, then,
would you cling
so tightly unto?

Servantship
is that which arises
when the death
of what could never possibly be
is irrevocably allowed.
It is the perfect heritage
extended from the Father
to the Son,
and is of one substance
with the Mystery
that our Heavenly Father is.

Servantship
requires only
the *enactment* of sacrifice,
that sacrifice which is,
from the beginning,
already completed:
the Grace of God.
Our choice to remember
who we are

is the enactment
of that sacrifice
already made in Heaven.

Sacrifice,
when completed,
gives rise to the birth of Love
both unconditional
and incomprehensible,
a Love which can only come
to be truly recognized
when any mind finally,
and irrevocably,
chooses to awaken
from the senseless dream
of the dreamer.

It is not a love tainted
by being directed
to the objects of the world,
nor felt only when a mind
momentarily perceives a satisfaction
born of the temporary *organization*
of the objects and events it embraces,
for no such love
is truly unconditional.
Therefore,
such love perceived
is not Love at all.
But what arises
is that self-same Love
that is already with us
from before time is,
the Love from which the
Son of God is birthed,

the Love which has already
fulfilled the Atonement
required by the brief —
and meaningless —
thought of separation.

It is that Love
which *is*
the very presence of God,
who is Love itself,
and *only* this.
Love seeks not for itself,
but finds its completion
in its eternal
and unreserved extension.

It is a Love
enacted by the Son
which unceasingly mirrors
the Love by which the Father
has begotten the Son.

It is a Love
which gives when asked
and holds nothing for itself.

It is a Love
that embraces all things,
for it sees no separation
in the whole of Creation.

It is a Love
that touches all who behold it
with a gentleness and certainty
whose taste is sweet above honey;

The Way of the Servant

it quenches the thirst of the soul.

And this,
without effort,
for it is a Love
that extends from —
and to —
true Being.

Seeing naught but the substance
of what alone is Real
in all that its eyes rest upon,
it severs with the sword of wisdom
the stranglehold of illusions
from the heart
of the one who beholds
the person of the arisen Christ.

It is not a Love
to be created,
but a Love that has finally
been allowed,
rising without resistance
from the soil of perfect surrender.

The dreamer,
vanquished and reborn,
decrees:
"I live,
yet not I,
but Christ,
dwells as me."

And the Word is made flesh,
and dwells among us.

Book Two

In the world,
but not of the world,
for the world is overcome
not by effort,
but by Grace . . .
the simple correction
of one mistaken perception.

Who, then,
is the servant?
What is she likened unto?

The servant is *free*.
No longer fettered
to the tiny fears
once seen as unscalable walls
reaching to block
the Light of the Son,
he loves not the things of the world,
for they hold no value.

The servant is *humble*.
No longer fettered
to the false arrogance
that once was made
to shield her from her aloneness,
she clings not to false knowledge,
for she knows that *she does not know*,
nor does she need to.
Trusting all things,
allowing all things,
she transcends all things

by first loving and embracing
all things.
And their passing
leaves not a trace upon her.

The servant is *capable*.
With no anxiety
for the things of tomorrow,
he enacts
the incomprehensible Love
of the Father *in this moment*.
Innocent as a child,
he considers not limitation,
for he sees with certainty that:

> *The works I do*
> *you also shall do,*
> *and greater works than these*
> *shall you do.*

He knows simply
that of himself he does nothing,
but the Father through him
does all things.
Where could incapacity arise?

Emptied of herself,
the servant effortlessly
dons the cloak
given her of the Father,
whether the cloak of this world
or another.
She moves freely
between Heaven and Earth,
rejoicing always

as the embodiment
of prayer without ceasing:
"Holy Father, *now* there is Light!"

The servant
is likened unto one
who has journeyed to a distant land,
for his master had commanded him:

> *Go, and share with all*
> *who have ears to hear*
> *and eyes to see.*
>
> *Give to them of my abundance,*
> *and give freely.*

Now,
when the servant heard,
she went immediately forth
and was found —
from waking to sleeping —
to be doing
as her master had asked.

And it came to pass
that many who received
secretly laughed
at the folly of the servant.
Many thought him mad,
and many more
either lost or discarded
what he shared with them.

Only a few,
having heard,

received what was given to them
and went and did likewise,
for in their hearing
they became like the servant,
and what they gave away
was returned to them tenfold.

So joyous in her task
was the servant
that she could hear not
the judgments of the small-minded.

Will you choose to have ears to hear?

The servant
is one who has
transcended history.

Quite literally,
she looks upon her past
and sees it, indeed,
as having passed away,
dissolved as mist
before the arising sun
from deep and forested valleys.
Not one dark corner remains
in the valleys of the mind,
cut and shaped by the forces
of limiting thought.

Rivers of radiant Light
flow unimpeded now,
emanating from the ocean of God's Love,
cascading waterfalls of vision
that embrace the whole of Creation.

Though disguised in simplicity,
the servant sees
his every loving gesture
touching the farthest star,
and participating in the miracle
of the Atonement.

The servant
always recognizes his own.
Herein is revealed
the true body of Christ,
the mystical Church
which far transcends
the loftiest of theologies.
Herein is revealed
the essence of brotherhood.

The servant
seeks out her own
and celebrates with them
without ceasing,
for awakened minds
are eternally joined as one.

The servant is *gentle.*
Clinging not
to what is not given her to do,
neither anger
nor impatience
arises.

The servant trusts.
Embracing all things,
having given the world
up to his Father,

The Way of the Servant

he is content in *this* moment.
The whole is present in the part,
and the part embraces the whole.
Forgetting not Heaven,
he blesses Earth,
and even his smile illuminates the world.

With nothing to do,
she does nothing.

With all things to do,
she accomplishes all things —
yet sees not a trace of distinction
between these.

The servant is at *peace*.
But more:
he is *peace*.

Receiving doubt,
he returns Love.
Receiving judgment,
she returns Love.
Receiving the projections of fear,
he returns Love.
Receiving love
not yet made wholly pure,
she returns Love.

Receiving Love
given purely,
he allows himself to receive it.

Abiding in unbroken union
with God,

she receives Love
without ceasing.

Though the world gives
and takes away,
his cup is always filled;
he drinks deeply with every breath.
Satiated,
he laughs at the world's illusions,
and his laughter heals the world.

The servant
is simply incomprehensible
to the perceptions of the world.
For where the world perceives lack,
the servant knows unlimited abundance.
Where the world perceives struggle,
the servant knows perfect harmony.
Where the world perceives
the pressure of time,
the servant knows the grace of eternity.

No reconciliation is possible,
for the things of Heaven and Earth
shall pass away,
but the things of God shall not.

And the first —
made so by the world —
shall be last.

The last —
being the creation of God —
shall again be made first
in the mind of the awakened

The Way of the Servant

joyous,
servant of God,
who is but Love.

As it was in the beginning,
is now,
and forever shall be.

What, then,
can the qualities
of genuine service
be likened unto?

Observe the waters
that flow from the highest mountains,
winding, cascading, twisting, churning,
resting inevitably in the sea.
Their destination
is neither hoped for, nor imagined.
It is *known*,
resting always in certainty.
And once the journey has begun,
the end is certain.

The river begins
as but a drop of rain
that falls from the heavens
freely given.
It forms itself in places unseen
and is shaped into a constant flow
that is not interrupted.

Seemingly shaped by the earth it touches,
it becomes the shaper of waterfalls
and canyons;
and what river of living waters
does not speak of beauty
to its beholder?

The river nurtures
all that it touches
with the very sustenance of Life.
It recognizes not obstacles to its journey,
but—
by embracing them—
overcomes them.
Even the sound of its passing
brings respite to those who listen.

It laments not
when others draw from it,
seemingly without gratitude,
for it knows its Source to be unlimited.
The secret of its peace,
and of its certain power, is this:
It already abides at one with the sea,
having arisen from it,
and returning always to it.

No veil of illusion
has arisen in its being
to create a sense of separation.
Therefore,
its journey begins in its certain end.

Let your service be given
like unto the rivers of life

The Way of the Servant

that flow from the highest mountains
to the sea.

Think not *you* must know
the nature of the journey,
nor that you must judge
whether the twists and turns
are acceptable.

For unto you there is given
the gift of one teacher
whose guidance never errs.
His Voice is certain,
his presence eternal.
Have I not said unto you:
"I will send you a Comforter?"

Yet,
the one whom I send
was received by me of our Father.
Because I have received Him,
He is given unto you equally.
Like an ancient melody,
his Voice is as a gentle song
at once familiar;
silence is the threshold
that carries the heart
to the inner chamber of the Holy One.

To give truly,
one must give all they have.
For to give
while holding one-part back
is to believe one has *not* all things.
And to she who believes she has not,

much will be taken,
while to she who knows she has all,
even more shall be added,
and her giving shall be unlimited
and without end.

She who gives all receives all.

The true servant gives even this:
all traces of attachment
to the fruit of her giving.
For her giving has been already seen
to be from the Father,
and so the fruits are given to her.

Thus the servant proclaims:
"Why do you call me good?
There is only one who is good:
God, who is but Love.
And if you would truly receive
what I would give you,
go, and do likewise."

Hear again:

He who gives all, receives all.

The servant
gives as he has been given,
but remembers it not.
Caring not for the accolades of the world,
he collects no ribbons,
and keeps no trophy.
But the face of Christ
seen in each he serves

The Way of the Servant

is etched in his awareness forever;
he remembers them
and gives thanks to the Father,
for the servant lives
the simplest of truths:

My brothers and sisters are my salvation.

The servant knows she fixes nothing.
Seeing not a fearful world,
she does not deliver it from "evil."
Looking not upon illness,
she calls not herself a healer.

Herein,
learn the secret of the miraculous:
The servant does nothing
save to extend Love
to the Christ who dwells in another,
having learned to see
past the appearances
that are the world;
and the one who is ill
recognizes that the servant
has recognized her
as she is, and decrees:
"I am seen as I AM,
and release my illusions now."

Love heals,
and Love alone.
Those unaccustomed to miracles
run after the servant, asking:
"How do you do these things?"

To which the servant replies:
"Love has done these things.
Of myself,
I only asked that my Father
correct my perception of you."

Love will flow through any mind
that asks for
and allows
the correction of its perceptions.

How, then,
does the servant serve?

By being *only* the presence of Love.

The extension of Love,
untainted by the thought of a doer,
is the quality of genuine service,
a reflection in this world
of the Love which begets eternally
the holy and only begotten child of God.

The Way of the Servant

Book Three

He who looks upon me.
and truly *sees* me,
has learned,
to look upon himself,
as our Father knows him.

She who sees me,
thus has she seen
the One who has sent me,
even as she, too,
has been sent of the Father
to proclaim but this:

> *Love alone is Real.*
> *God is but Love.*
> *Therefore,*
> *God is.*

Herein lies the meaning of my words,
read often,
yet often not understood:

> *It is not possible*
> *for what is Real to be threatened,*
> *nor is it possible*
> *for what is unreal to exist.*

Because you know only that you exist,
you must be in God,
and cannot be threatened
in any way.
Nor does the illumined mind
behold the place where it begins
and God ends.

The Way of the Servant

For what alone is Real
is without beginning or end.

Yet,
always does such a mind
recognize that it is created,
and not Creator,
knowing not the unfathomable Source
of its beginning.

This recognition
is the seat of humility.
Humility begets
the recognition of freedom,
and in perfect freedom
lies true power:

> *I can do absolutely nothing,*
> *nor need I do anything,*
> *for the One who has sent me*
> *alone does all things.*

Joy flows gently from the heart
of one who has awakened.

It is a joy
neither created nor possessed,
but *allowed*.
Flowing as the radiant extension
of a Light that meets no obstacle,
it attracts those
who would choose to Remember,
and behold themselves reflected
in the one who has awakened.

Book Three

When you see me
in the face of your brother and sister,
you become the mirror
of their only Reality,
and in *you* can they know Christ.

Therefore,
your relationship with each of them
is the means of your salvation,
and your only appropriate gift to them
is to be one who has refused to tolerate
the error of separation
in yourself,
offering to them the gift of *their* perfect —
and holy —
reflection.

The holiest place on Earth is, indeed,
wherever an ancient hatred
has become a present love.
Hatred is ancient,
being born of separation;
having a beginning,
it must have an end.

Love,
being of God,
knows neither beginning nor end.
To offer your brother and sister
the gift of your holiness
is to offer the gift of what is eternal.
Eternity must speak to them of Grace,
and by Grace and Grace alone
the world is overcome.

The Way of the Servant

Join with me
and offer our friends
the holiness
you share with me
from before the foundations
of the world.

Nothing beyond this
can be found,
and in this
there is nothing lacking.
All searching has ended,
and in what is eternal
there can be nothing you want still.

In giving your Self,
you must remember your Self.
This alone
is the straight and narrow path,
the bridge given you when,
in a distant and forgotten past,
you looked upon one insane thought,
and failed to laugh.

Your seriousness
made the insanity of separation
seem real to you.
Gone now is all fear,
for we see together
that what is unreal
cannot possibly exist.

Now,
we are safe.

Book Three

Now,
peace has come.
Giving this alone to everyone,
we have received it forever.

The servant gives,
and therefore receives.

I have said
that I come to gather my friends
to myself.

Gather those who are given to you,
and it is enough.
And because you have received
the ones I send to you
in order that they might behold
in your holiness
their true reflection,
verily,
you have received me.
And our friendship must be eternal,
being established in God.

When I said,
"Go, and do likewise,"
it is just this
to which I was referring.

> *For as many as received Him,*
> *gave He the power to become*
> *the Sons and Daughters*
> *of the Living God.*

This can only mean

that when you give the gift
of your holiness,
you have paid witness to the truth
that you *have* received me.

Because you have allowed me
to raise you from the dead,
you are the one
in whom I now live,
and the only logical meaning
of the Second Coming
is witnessed by those
who are given to you.

If but one of our precious friends
sees that I live in you,
the whole of Creation is uplifted.

You are sent forth "in my name"
to extend the power to awaken
unto all who will be sent to you,
and in you will they be provided
with the opportunity to see themselves
as they are held eternally
in the mind of God.

Remember
that in the Kingdom
there is no effort.
Because you are awake in me,
you need do nothing,
yet not one thing
shall be left undone.
And what I ask of you,
you will accomplish,

because our wills are joined.

It is not possible that you fail,
for this would mean
that God has failed me,
and my Father fails not his Son.

The choice for Love,
which is the end of fear,
is the choice to see
with the eyes of Christ:

> *God has not failed me,*
> *and I cannot fail those*
> *who are sent to me,*
> *because the One who has sent me*
> *lives in me.*

Giving them to God —
by seeing that Christ is in them —
they are received *through* me,
but *by* God,
who receives his own.

All praise to the One
beyond all comprehension!
I am *not* the doer,
I am *not* the maker.
I AM
but the humble servant,
allowing
the witnessing of Love in me,
because Christ lives in me.
And this is enough.
What perfection the world reveals!

The Way of the Servant

What sublime beauty
do all things show me!

My joy
is beyond measure,
my pleasure unending!

Weariness is gone,
and the dance begun.

The song of the One
in whom I dwell
lifts me gently in dancing!

The leaves tossed in the wind,
the laughter of a child,
the radiance of the farthest star,
each one who stands before me,
these are the partners
with whom I dance!

Perfection shines forth
in all things;
the weaver of the dance is trusted.

If I am with you in this moment,
we dance as friends in holiness,
for we cannot fail to be
where God has asked us to be.

The eternal melody shifts,
and moves on.
I dance with the one sent unto me,
yet lose not the one
who appears to have gone.

Book Three

For minds that have joined in Love
can in no way be separate,
one from another.

Fail not to dance, oh holy Son of God!
Know you not what comes to pass?

The crucifixion is past,
the resurrection completed,
and ascension now descends upon us
as a gentle dove,
lifting us to the abode
of the One who is but Love!

Forget you not to dance
with every breath you breathe,
for Love waits upon your welcome,
and desires to be heard
with every spoken word!

You are the one sent forth from God!
You are the one
in whom He remains
eternally well pleased!
You are the one in whom I live,
and reveal myself to the world!
You, precious friend,
you are as I AM!
In your joyousness
is my laughter heard.
In your giving
am I received.

Dance you therefore with passion,
not for the things of the world,

The Way of the Servant

but for that which alone is Real
and cannot be taken from us.

Because Light
is reborn in *you*,
your brothers and sisters rejoice!
You have become their salvation
and they, yours.
Their gratitude is joined with mine,
and our voices are raised as one:
"God *is*!"

The ancient melody is heard,
the sacred and happy dance enjoined.
Because we dance,
we *do* know what comes to pass.

We are the bringers of Heaven to Earth,
that the things of the world
might be forgotten,
and the purpose of time
might be completed.

The translation
of a brief and harmless dream
is finished,
and all things are quietly returned.

The Sonship is remembered as One
and the first, is first,
eternally.

The field of obstacles
through which the dreamer stumbles
are but various symbols

of the one thing
he seems to have created in error.
For appearances are error
and nothing more.

I have often said —
in many ways
and through many channels —
that there is but one lesson
you need learn:

There is nothing outside you.

As with all expressions of wisdom,
this statement is true
at many levels.

Levels appear to exist
as long as the dream seems to remain.
Because you are awake,
the idea of levels
no longer pertains to you.

Therefore,
the "secret" of this work
is now revealed;
it is given to those
who are the teachers of God,
for only they will truly
and clearly
understand it.

In knowing that they
do understand it,
they will know they have received

the "sign from Heaven"
I once promised them.
Now
they are free
to take up their cross
and follow me,
for where I have gone
they now can come.
And the whole thought structure
of the world
has been reversed in them.

Because it is completed in them,
it shall quickly be completed
in the entire Sonship.

This are they certain of,
and our voices are raised as one.

All things perceived
arise only within the mind.
Because all minds are joined,
whatever is perceived has arisen
in *one* mind,
shared equally by all.

To say "all minds are joined"
is to say only that there is one mind,
and the things of Heaven and Earth
arise
and pass away
within it.

Book Three

You have learned
that the body's senses
have led you to believe
that everything
beyond the boundary
of the body
is outside you.
But you have recognized
that *this cannot be true.*

It has always made sense to you
that your thoughts are not outside you.
It has required great courage
to learn the truth
that your brother's or sister's thought
is *also not outside* you.

Until recently,
you have remained fearful
of taking the next logical step.
While just a few traces of guilt remained
you have feared what you perceived
as an overwhelming responsibility.

But because the Father
has taken the final step for you,
you abide in the perfect safety
where the next step
is no longer fearful.

I have said that the Holy Spirit
never teaches you
what you are still
fearful of learning.
Because of this,

two things follow.

First:
Before you chose
to be awake in me,
it appeared that a prayer
could fail to be answered.
This was because you feared
receiving the answer,
and so it was not given you.
But what you were willing to receive
always *was* given.

Now,
because you are willing
to receive all,
all *is* given you.
Yet,
because your eyes are open,
you no longer pray
"in vain."
This means only
that you have gone beyond
the childish prayers for those things
you once believed you needed
to save you
from what you thought you feared.
Because fear is gone,
childish prayer has vanished.

Awake in our Remembrance,
you have learned to pray
only for the Atonement of the Sonship,
and have extended to me
your willingness to join with me

in answering the only true prayer.

This has required
the re-learning of trust,
and trust is the inevitable fruit
of the forgiveness
you have extended to the world,
of which you are a worthy part.

This willingness
has given me permission
to dismantle the "mansions"
you had made in error;
every teacher of God
has faced crucifixion.

Through forgiveness,
and mastery
of the keys to the Kingdom,
you have passed through
the eye of the needle
to join me in the resurrection.
All things *have* been made new again!

Second:
Because you are now taking
the next step,
it must mean that the fear
which had kept
what you prayed for from you
is *no longer present*.
This can only mean
that my promise has been kept:
I have given you my strength
until yours has become

as certain as mine.
Because you know that I live in you,
your strength is as certain as mine,
and the next step
we can now take together.

For those who have chosen
to learn this curriculum
through my *Course in Miracles,*
you will clearly remember
that it was not designed
to answer every question
a teacher of God might have.
It could not do so,
being only a teaching device
aimed at a specific goal:
peace.

Peace is the necessary foundation
from which the teacher of God
moves to complete the Atonement
on Earth,
as it is already completed in Heaven.

Now
are we ready
to take the necessary step,
and accept the final meaning
of the one lesson:

There is nothing outside you.

You are your brother's keeper
because you are your brother.

Book Three

The translation
of the unhappy dream of separation
into the final,
happy dream —
the final manifestation in time —
requires that it be accomplished
through you.

Those of you
who understand clearly
the meaning of this work
are those in whom all preparation
is completed.
You have learned
that the purpose of your life
is *exactly the same as was mine,*
to demonstrate that, with God,
all things are not simply possible,
but inevitable.
You are now ready
to become a *living demonstration*
of *complete mastery.*

Because all resistance is gone
(for what is ego but this?),
the discipline necessary
for the completion of your demonstration
is as an "easy yoke."
It is a discipline
that must joyfully touch
upon every aspect of your life.

It is through you
that the simple and natural righteousness
of God's "laws"

can be demonstrated.

Mastery in *every* aspect
of the life given unto you
is the only way you can teach
your brother and your sister
that God *is*.

This means that now
we look together
beyond the mind's tendency
to separate itself from the world
by looking upon aspects of life
not yet mastered,
and decreeing them to be simply illusions.
While this is true,
it is not appropriate to conclude
that they be left untransformed.

To those with ears to hear:
It is simply not possible to transcend
what you refuse to acknowledge
and embrace.
Denial is but the ploy of ego
to ensure that your Self
remains imprisoned,
and *the ego* remains enthroned.

Again I ask of you:

*What do you **want**, truly?*

Book Four

The Way of the Servant

Book Four

Self-mastery and servantship.
are one.
For where one is, the other is found.
And Where the other is,
the one is also known.

Mastery is that state
in which not one thing of the world
compels you in any direction,
yet not one thing of the world is judged.
This must naturally follow
for the mind to which peace is returned.

To lack mastery
in any aspect of life
is to lack it in all.

Mastery
is the foundation from which
the servant enacts
the movement of Love
proceeding from the Father
through the Son,
serving the one goal of Atonement
by demonstrating its completion
in you.

This is given
as a clear sign unto you:
Mastery is completed when not one habit
learned of the world remains;
not one "love"
you have miscreated for yourself

is justified of you.

Look well, then,
at the whole of your life,
and behold with innocent honesty
the "loves" you would keep for yourself,
for what can you carry forth
from death to Life?
Even the body will be outshined.

And if you love the Father
above the world,
what would you leave untransformed
by the radiance of your union?

You can give
only what you possess,
and what you possess exists for you
only because you value it.

What treasure
will you lay at your brother's feet?
For where your treasure is,
there shall your heart be also,
and your heart is all that *can* be given.

I have said before
that the world is but a *symbol*.
Choose wisely what *your* world
will symbolize for you,
for it is the symbols you choose
which your sister will see.
Thus is your heart revealed,
and you have "spoken" your judgment
of the Father.

Book Four

She who knows me
walks with me,
and she who walks with me
makes straight her path,
and all things are given
to the praise of what God is:
Love.

Love embraces all things,
heals all things,
transforms all things,
celebrates all things,
and, above all,
mirrors what God is *in* all things.

Give no thought, then,
for tomorrow,
neither for the things you shall eat,
nor for the things you shall wear,
for the Father knows you have need
of these things,
and He will not leave you comfortless.

When I once asked you
to "take no thought"
you unwittingly failed to hear me,
deciding *you* can direct the choice
of what you would eat,
and what you would wear,
and thus cleverly cherish
the "loves" you would desire to keep.
To decide for yourself
is precisely to *take* thought.
That is,
because you failed

to let the Comforter choose for you,
right-mindedness was cast aside,
and the real world abandoned.

But she
who praises God in *all* things
keeps no decision for herself,
listening only to the Voice for God,
and the servant knows
the Voice speaks only
with perfect reason.
To cling to but one "love"
you have miscreated
is surely to be unreasonable,
for you have learned
that the symbols of the world
can be but the symbols of death.
Death is no longer your will,
but Life.

I am come again unto you
that you might have Life,
and this more abundantly.
Learn well, then,
to ask before each choice:
"Does this value the symbols of death,
or of Life?"

Abiding in innocent honesty,
you will realize
that the Comforter's guidance
is immediate,
and uncompromising.

Book Four

Herein will be revealed to you
the final meaning of my teaching:

> *Take no thought,*
> *for the Father knows*
> *you have need of these things.*

In this,
the next step *has* been taken.

Released from the insane belief in sacrifice
and loss,
not a single "love"
does the servant keep for himself.

Knowing
with a certainty beyond question
who walks with him
in the way that he chooses to go,
he steps with gentle authority
on the path set before him.

Caring not for what she will wear
nor for what she shall eat,
she listens for the Voice
of the Holy One.

Because her prayer is only
for that which can reflect
the Father's perfect Love through her,
her joy is forever complete.
And the Comforter's guidance
is without reproach,
revealing the gifts
that are brought to serve

the one desire that alone arises
in the holy mind of the servant:

That all I do
and all I say,
that all I think
and all I share,
that all I be, do, and have,
reflect the radiance,
the joy,
the grace,
the laughter,
the compassion,
the power,
the vision,
and the mastery
of my Father's one creation:
Christ, I AM!

And the things that she wears
and the things that she eats
whisper to the world
of the Love with which the Father
has restored his precious child
to her rightful place.

Whenever you are not wholly joyous,
it is because you have chosen wrongly.
For from choice there follows action,
and from action always experience.
For those with ears to hear,
let them hear:
He who has learned that death is unreal

gladly releases the symbols of death
even within the illusions of time,
down to the least jot and tittle.

The awakened servant,
having truly chosen
to teach *only* Love
because Love alone is desired,
moves from the silent foundation of union
unto Life *everlasting,*
teaching only the symbols of Life,
for by teaching he learns
and by giving he receives.

The Way, then,
is easy,
and without effort.

From the thoughts
you would choose to think,
to what you would eat
and what you would wear,
take no thought of yourself,
but receive the guidance
of the One sent unto you of the Father,
because He has loved you
from before the foundation of *all* worlds.

Herein,
while time seems to last for you,
are all things translated
into that which reflects
the holy of holies,
and what was hidden is now revealed.

The Way of the Servant

I gave even the body
that it might be glorified
in glad tribute to my Father.
For she who gives all,
receives all.

Remember then,
what I say unto you now:
If your brother is hungry,
you are without nourishment,
and if your sister is alone,
you are separated from the feast.
Because there is
nothing outside you,
you are the good shepherd.
And I ask only for you
to accept the truth
that because you have chosen
to awaken to your own call,
the time is at hand
for embracing with me
all that is given you,
that the world
might be restored in us,
the holy, unlimited,
and *only* begotten child of God.

If you will do this with me,
all things *will* be embraced,
and Love will light all things.
Be you, therefore, of good courage.
Love one another
as I love you, always.
Rejoice,
and celebrate with one another often,

for if there are two or more
gathered together to embrace the world,
I *am* in the midst of them.

We walk now with certainty,
holding not one "love"
back from the teacher
who would heal all wounds,
and translate even the body —
the symbol of ego —
into that which reflects only Light
to a world redeemed
from the dream of separation.

The final lesson has been learned,
and now will be gladly lived:

There is nothing outside me.

Now, it is finished.

He who understands these words,
lives them,
and his life is a dance of devotion
without ceasing,
unlimited forever,
for he knows what comes to pass.

The happy dream dawns now,
having been placed safely within you
by God himself
even as you were —
for but one brief moment —
distracted by a tiny, mad idea.

The Way of the Servant

My peace
I give unto you.
Not as the world gives,
do I give unto you.
Because you have received me,
you give me to the world.
Because you give me,
do you eternally receive me,
forever,
and ever.

Peace be unto you,
beloved,
precious,
and ancient
friend.

Amen

After Words

After Words

Now is the end come.
We are returned,
to the ancient beginning.

Here,
Where Truth is restored,
We look with gentleness
Upon the world.

The Way of the Servant

You are here only to be
truly helpful.
Yet
you do not know
what needs to be done.

Would you know
your Father's will for you?

Precious friend,
open the eyes of your Self;
it will not be hidden
from you.

After Words

Where does the servant go,
awakened to the eternal?

"Here,"
comes the quiet reply.

The Way of the Servant

Because *you*,
are awake *here*,
and your sister
is awake *here*,
though bodies are
seemingly separate,
there is not two,
but one.

Pray,
　fast,
meditate.
Journey into the silent places
of your precious Earth,
for she alone is your mother.

Sing,
laugh,
dance,
play.

Drink the first rays of a new dawn.
Touch the dark velvet
of a moonless night.
Feel the grasses against your skin,
and stand beneath
the cascading waterfall.

Give but one day of your week
to silence,
eating only the Light
from your Father.

The Way of the Servant

Smile often,
and remember,
you have chosen to come,
here.
Look around you,
and bless the place you are.
Do these things often,
in remembrance of me.

After Words

I AM

with

you

always . . .

Epilogue

LOVE. It *does* ride on every breath we breathe, and over the course of this experience with Jeshua, I have learned that Love *does* desire to be heard with every single spoken word. Jeshua is a master of it, but his mastery does not place Him above us. He will wait patiently, perhaps perceived as a little ahead of us, until we recognize that what awaits us, what has *always* awaited us, is the choice for Love. It is a choice in which all other options collapse, a choice which, in the final analysis, is actually revealed to our awakened minds as the *choiceless choice*. Has there ever been any other viable option?

Love can seem so frightening! It requires the deep recognition that the past is *passed away*. It requires that we come home to *this* present moment, relinquishing our need to be right, our penchant for blaming, and above all, claiming complete responsibility for everything we think, feel, say, and do. It also must come to mean that we accept responsibility *for the world we see*. If the world isn't changing, we must not be changing!

The spoken word. Not merely verbal communication, for *we are the thought of Love in form*. Our every gesture, then, "speaks" to the world of what we are choosing to lay up as our treasures. But more than this, our every gesture speaks also to us, whispering what our choice has been, and *offering the perfect freedom to choose again*.

Together, we stand now on the threshold of something new, something unparalleled, at least in known history. The pulse of change is everywhere felt. Technology is making the world a very small place, indeed. In an instant, the experience of a brother or sister living on the other side of the globe is brought into our living room,

Their voices compelling us to stretch our hearts wide, to accept them, too, as true family. Can *we* love enough? No, I think not. But, thank *God*, Love itself is enough, for surely God *is* Love, waiting on our welcome.

In nearly twenty years, as this PathWay we now call the Way of Mastery has unfolded under His meticulous guidance, I have seen time and time again the undeniable truth that there really is no order of difficulty in the miracles Love can bring forth, when we simply join our hearts and hands and offer Love the tiny bit of willingness it takes to suspend our judgments and learn anew. Oh, yes, Love is enough. Beneath every denied feeling, beneath every anger and hurt we cling to, Love waits to heal us so deeply that it seems the "problem" was never there, as though we slept for a while, and dreamt dreams of loss, of weakness, of unworthiness, of guilt, of shame, of unreality. What joy to awaken!

We *are* awakening. We—you and I and everyone—have been together as long as time has been. We have dreamt together every dream unlike Love, and the choiceless choice comes to present itself yet again. We are the makers of the world we see, and this recognition can seem to paralyze us, depress us, or immobilize us, until we realize that it is only an expression of the thoughts we have insisted on maintaining as real! We are free now, free to *choose again*.

Jeshua has been an enigma for 2,000 years. That is a long time to be famous, especially without building an empire, writing any books, or being allowed as a subject of study in public schools. The guy doesn't have any movie credits to his name, nor did He ever invent anything. But He did accept the choiceless choice to *live* the reality of Love. And that has made all the difference—for Him, and for everyone who has ever opened their heart just a little to Him. He has often said that He has waited long for *this* time to be present on the Earth. A time when a timeless Truth can be breathed as an idea into minds and hearts, and spread rapidly and completely around the world. I say "breathed" because the time for dogma, for preaching, is behind us. To *breathe* the truth first requires that we take it deeply into ourselves, literally with every breath, then offer it to whoever is in front of us, literally with each outward breath, as though bathing them in what is beyond words. We can invite them, in an atmosphere of safety, to breathe with us. It can become a circle, a dance, of receiving and giving, giving and receiving. Are we willing to initiate such sharing?

When we make the choiceless choice for Love, right *here* and right *now*, wherever we are, we join with others all over the world who are also choosing to awaken. Our every loving gesture literally uplifts the world, because it must necessarily affect the collective mind of mankind.

One of my favorite quotes is from a Jewish teacher, Maimonidies. What he asks is perhaps the only question we need answer. While it points to our responsibility, it also points to the immeasurable power that lives *equally* within each of us, and will shine forth as we unlearn our fear of it. The question is this:

If not NOW, when?
If not YOU, who?

With Jeshua as loving brother and guide, we have learned that the choiceless choice is the inevitable recognition that the *when* is now, and the *who* is us. We have also learned that awakening is not about some ephemeral aloofness masquerading as transcendence, in which every challenge and every unwanted feeling is explained away as an illusion. Rather, awakening is a *correction*, a wiping clean of the slate of learned perceptions, so that life, which is but Love extending itself to embrace creation, can finally be *lived* and not merely survived. It is not an end, but a beginning. My friend, Michael Stillwater, calls it "landing with your feet on the planet."

"Beam me up, Scottie" is *not* what our gentle brother teaches, nor lives for. Love does not seek escape, but serves. While the ego cries out, "But what is in it for me?" the awakened heart asks simply, "How can I help?"... then lets Love be the guide.

Alan Cohen wrote that "Jeshua would probably agree that we have had enough students, and it is time for more masters." I wholeheartedly agree. He has never asked to be worshipped, only to be joined. Love will prevail in the end, if only because it requires great energy to resist it, and that resistance will finally exhaust itself.

We learn either through joy or through pain, but we *will* learn. The direction of the wise choice seems obvious enough.

Jeshua once stopped me in my tracks by saying that "the truths of the world are *diametrically opposed* to the Reality of the Kingdom." That means that everything we have been taught is the exact opposite of what is real! The world has taught us that we must know where we are going before starting the journey. We must know what we are going to get, how it is going to affect us, and then decide whether or not to launch our ship. We need to make sure we have our parachute in order before we jump. *But exactly the opposite is true!*

I believe in you. I believe that you are intimately united with the Source of Life, and that Life longs to be lived through *you*;

Epilogue

that you have every right to set aside the ways of this world, where the laws of chaos, distrust, and fear seem to rule. If you jump, you will find your parachute. To all of you who have jumped, and to the growing number of us who are now moving to the edge, I extend our gratitude to you for being willing to join with everyone now choosing to bring Heaven to Earth.

Well, there. Now that it is 5 a.m., I can crawl back under the covers. Something more needed to be shared to complete this book. I see now that Jeshua, throughout *The Way of the Servant*, was both correcting our collective misconceptions about who we really are, while also asking Maimonides' question. A question waits on an answer, and I could not let this edition go to press without answering it. Here, then, is my final offering to you. May we join together to grow, heal, and push the limits of awakening. May we join to envision a planet healed and a humanity at peace, and to do all we can to share who we really are—radical, ecstatic spirit—together with what we can discover that is truly helpful with those who will be drawn to us!

Heaven on Earth.

Jeshua refers to this as the "adamic process" . . . "Dam" in his native Aramaic language refers to nature, or the bodymind itself.

"A" (pronounced Aaahh) is the first letter of the name for God he used the most: "Alaha," and signifies the unlimited source we have come to call "God."

Thus, "a" seeks to penetrate, suffuse, and move through "dam," as it seeks in the great cycle of evolution to manifest what has not yet completed its full birthing: "Adam" the "first man" of the bible! For we are all part of this great birthing as the fullness of real humanity.

    Can there be a greater adventure?
    Can there be anything more worthy of our being?

Streams of joy!
Jayem
Easter, 2006

A PRAYER OF REMEMBRANCE

Father-Mother God,
　　Source of our Being,
we are returned,

Joining together,
we celebrate the Love that,
together, we are.

Where there has been an unreal world,
we now give birth to a world atoned,
that it may perfectly reflect
what you have completed in us.

Because we are made,
even in this moment,
in your image,
our love is without ceasing,
forever, and ever, and ever!

Amen

WayofMasteryBooks.com
Book Catalog

All New releases will be announced on the website as well as access to Kindle/ eReader versions and special audio offerings

IN BOOKSTORES

The Way *of* Heart
The Christ Mind Trilogy
Volume I

The *Way of the Heart* is the first of *The Christ Mind Trilogy* teachings, the core, formal, lessons of *The Way of Mastery* Pathway.

The lessons here are ones that Jeshua Himself was given in His lifetime, and subjects include the nature and meaning of reality, the power of forgiveness, purified desire as alignment to the Will of God, the four "Keys to the Kingdom," and much more.

The Way of the Heart teachings and experiential learnings provides the firm and essential foundation for all of that which follows in *The Christ Mind Trilogy*. It is a key aspect of Jeshua's Pathway of Enlightenment, and His Promise to us to help us awaken from the illusion that we have ever been separate from God, and to remember the deepest Truth of who we are: Christ.

ISBN 978-1-941489-41-3
Available in Paperback, Hardcover, Kindle, eReader & Audiobook

IN BOOKSTORES

The Way *of* Transformation
The Christ Mind Trilogy
Volume II

The Way of Transformation is the second of The Christ Mind Trilogy teachings, or the 'Way of' Lessons. These were originally recorded as live channelings of Jeshua, and later transcribed. Together, the trilogy forms an in-depth three year Course in *The Way of Mastery* devoted to healing the illusions that bind us beyond mere 're-training' of the mind. It is meant to be read and studied only after the student has completed *The Way of the Heart* text and lessons.

Hear what Jeshua says of it:

"The Way of Transformation absolutely requires that you be committed to living differently. For is not transformation a change from the status quo? How can you experience transformation if you do not use time to think and be differently? Crying out to me will not do it. Reading a thousand holy books will not do it. One thing, and one thing only, will bring you into the transformation that you have sought — the willingness to abide where you are, differently."

The Way of Transformation teachings and experiential learnings provide the firm and critical foundation for *The Way of Knowing*, the final part of *The Christ Mind Trilogy*.

ISBN 978-1-941489-42-0
Available in Paperback, Hardcover, Kindle, eReader & Audiobook

IN BOOKSTORES

The Way *of* Knowing
The Christ Mind Trilogy
Volume III

The Way of Knowing is the third and final teaching of *The Christ Mind Trilogy*, a Course originally recorded as live channelings of Jeshua over a three year period, and foundational to the larger Way of Mastery Pathway. It is meant to be read and studied only after the student has completed *The Way of the Heart* and *The Way of Transformation* texts and lessons. In Jeshua's own words:

"*In The Way of Knowing, the final surrender* is entered — that surrender which is beyond the comprehension of all the languages and theologies of your world, beyond all that can be spoken or uttered, yet not what can be *known, felt, realized, and lived!*"

Here, He unequivocally tells us that what we consider as 'knowledge' is a pale substitute for the mystical transfiguration the Christ Path is truly devoted to:

"Knowledge is a knowing by being that which is known."

Following the completion of the *Christ Mind Trilogy*, Jeshua begins the astounding restoration of His original Aramaic Teachings, notably the Lords Prayer and Beatitudes, along with a one year online Course for the maturing student called *Jewels of the Christ Mind*.

ISBN 978-1-941489-43-7
Available in Paperback, Hardcover, Kindle, eReader & Audiobook

IN BOOKSTORES

The Jeshua Letters
A Remarkable Encounter with Christ

In July 1987, Jesus (Jeshua) appeared out of a field of light, fully formed, to his chosen channel and scribe Jayem. Over a period of nearly two years Jeshua appeared many times and gave 'dictation', which Jayem recorded, and which became the earliest parts of *The Way of Mastery Pathway*. Eventually Jeshua asked that these be published, and they, along with Jayem's personal reflections on how all this unfolded, make up *The Jeshua Letters*.

The Jeshua Letters is the start of an astounding body of work given by Jeshua which restore the essential truths of His original teachings, previously 'lost in translation' in their passage from Aramaic to English. Jeshua's 'Letters' are simple, profound and practical. His voice is certain but always gentle; inviting, never demanding. To read them is know beyond doubt - to know palpably - that Truth is being expressed.

ISBN 978-1-941489-45-1 • *Available in Paperback, Hardcover, Kindle, eReader*

IN BOOKSTORES

The Way of the Servant

The Way of the Servant is the second text dictated by Jeshua and scribed by Jayem in *The Way of Mastery Pathway*, following The Jeshua Letters.

Jeshua oftens speaks of "beginning at the end", and here He does so, showing us nothing less than how the Pathway flowers as the highest pinnacle of Consciousness (fully realized Christ Mind) that can be known in this world: *true servantship*, devoted to the realization of Humanity's highest evolution or, the 'coming of heaven to earth'.

Short, succinct, of extraordinary mystical depth, countless Pathway students find that immersing in *Way of the Servant* every year reveals depths and brings illuminations they were incapable of truly comprehending before!

ISBN 978-1-941489-44-4 • Available in Paperback, Hardcover, Kindle, eReader

IN BOOKSTORES

The
Early Years
Volume I
Now, We Begin

The Early Years (volumes I & II) are transcriptions of gatherings recorded live as Jeshua taught us all. The wisdom, guidance, and sheer brilliance of them is astounding; there is so much in these pages, dear reader, that will help you grow in understanding, support you to truly heal into peace, and more!

Volume one includes the talks below:
- Awakening
- Choose to See
- Death Earth Changes
- Decide to be Christ
- Grace as Reality
- Healing
- Heaven on Earth
- Ignorance is Bliss
- Joy I
- Joy II

ISBN 978-1-941489-46-8 • *Available in Paperback, Hardcover, Kindle, eReader*

IN BOOKSTORES

The Early Years
Volume II
Now, We Begin

The Early Years (volumes I & II) are transcriptions of gatherings recorded live as Jeshua taught us all. The wisdom, guidance, and sheer brilliance of them is astounding; there is so much in these pages, dear reader, that will help you grow in understanding, support you to truly heal into peace, and more!

Volume two includes the talks below:
- Mastering Communication
- The Blessing of Forgiveness
- The Divine Feminine
- The Holy Instant
- The Holy Spirit
- The Light that You are
- Walk with Me
- Love Heals All Things
- The Meaning of Ascension
- Teach Only Love
- The Heart of Freedom
- The Master of Time

ISBN 978-1-941489-47-5 • *Available in Paperback, Hardcover, Kindle, eReader*

COMING SOON

Darshan

Over a period of 3 years, originally in live group video recordings, Jayem offered for the first time an in depth immersion into each lesson of The Way of Mastery Christ Mind Trilogy. He reveals the rich beauty and practical wisdom of the Teachings and shares transforming insights into their timeless Lessons, garnered from his own studentship of them for over some 25 years.

This is a remarkable and vast treasure trove of material, and we anticipate 6-8 volumes as we transcribe over 178 hours of audio into written form.

COMING SOON

The Later Years

While Jeshua guided Jayem deeply into the Aramaic Teachings and their application to the students transformation, He ceased public channelings. Then, in 2010 He abruptly stated it was to begin again at a Pathway gathering in England, where He announced the 'Turning of the Ages'.

Also, gathered here, are some of the promised messages from other Teachers of the Lineage, notably Mary Magdalene and Elijah.

COMING SOON

The Living Practices
The Alchemy of Living from The True Heart

Well beyond the *Christ Mind Trilogy,* Jeshua –over a several year period – revealed the profound methods of healing the roots of Separation while cultivating the ground of mystical consciousness, and restored His original teachings utilized by the Essenes, as given in the Beatitudes and Lords Prayer. Principally, these are LovesBreath and Radical Inquiry. Here, find a rich and practical treasure trove of genuine transformative practices meant to also be utterly practical in our daily lives.

COMING SOON

The Christ Mind Trilogy
Spanish Edition

The Christ Mind Trilogy in 3 volumes will be published in Spanish and we are anticipating a 4th quarter release date. Keep an eye out at WayofMasteryBooks.Com for updated release dates on all our upcoming additions.

COMPLIMENTARY READING

The Essene Gospel of Peace

For the first time the complete 4 books of the Essene Gospel of Peace are available in one volume.

- *The Essene Gospel of Peace*
- *The Unknown Book of the Essenes*
- *Lost Scrolls of the Essene Brotherhood*
- *The Teachings of the Elect.*

The Essene Gospel of Peace were found in the Vatican Library and translated by Edmond Bordeaux Szekely

Edmond Bordeaux Szekely, grandson of Alexandre Szekely, eminent poet and Unitarian Bishop of Cluj, is a descendant of Csoma de Koros, Transylvanian traveler and philologist who, over 150 years ago, compiled the first grammar of the Tibetan language, the first English-Tibetan dictionary, and wrote his unsurpassed work, Asiatic Researches. He was also Librarian to the Royal Asiatic Society in India. Dr. Bordeaux earned his Ph. D. degree from the University of Paris, and other degrees from the Universities of Vienna and Leipzig. He also held professorships of Philosophy and Experimental Psychology at the University of Cluj. A well-known philologist in Sanscrit, Aramaic, Greek and Latin, Dr. Bordeaux spoke ten modern languages.

In 1928, he founded the International Biogenic Society with Nobel Prize-winning author, Romain Rolland. His most important translations, in addition to selected texts from the Dead Sea Scrolls and the Essene Gospel of Peace over a million copies in 26 languages are selected texts from the Zend Avesta and from pre Columbian codices of ancient Mexico. His last works on the Essene Way of Biogenic Living have attracted worldwide interest. He is the author of more than 80 books published in many countries on philosophy and ancient cultures.

ISBN 978-1-941489-40-6 • *308 pages, Paperback*

www.ingramcontent.com/pod-product-compliance
Lightning Source LLC
LaVergne TN
LVHW041338080426
835512LV00006B/518